# Why Is This Festival Special?

# Christmas

## Jillian Powell

**W**

FRANKLIN WATTS
LONDON • SYDNEY

This edition 2009

Franklin Watts
338 Euston Road
London NW1 3BH

Franklin Watts Australia
Level 17/207 Kent Street
Sydney, NSW 2000

Copyright © Franklin Watts 2005

Series editor: Sarah Peutrill
Art director: Jonathan Hair
Picture researcher: Diana Morris
Design: Ian Thompson
Consultant: Martin Ganeri O.P.

A CIP catalogue record for this book is available from the
British Library.

ISBN: 978 0 7496 9013 7
Dewey classification number: 394.26'63

Printed in Malaysia

Picture credits: Alpix: 21t. APL/ArkReligion: 20b. Bill
Bachman/ImageWorks/Topham: 24t. Peter Barker/Eye
Ubiquitous: 22b. Sean Clayton/ImageWorks/Topham: 12. Andy
Crawford: 15. Bob Daemmrich/ImageWorks/Topham: 6. Jeff
Greenberg/ImageWorks/Topham: 25t, 26b. E. James/ArkReligion:
13b. Mary Jeliffe/ArkReligion: 18. Perry Joseph: 17b. Nancy Durrell
Mckenna/Hutchison: 17t. Jef Maion/Nomad's Land/Alamy: 25b.
Ray Moller/Franklin Watts: cover b, 10t, 11, 14, 20t, 21c, 21b, 23,
24b. Picturepoint/Topham: 26c. Helene Rogers/ArkReligion: 7b, 8.
Steve Mary Skjold/Eye Ubiquitous: 27. Liba Taylor/Hutchison:
front cover t. A.Tjagny-rjadno/ArkReligion: 19b. Topham: 7t.
World Religions Picture Library: 3, 9bl, 9tr, 10b, 13t, 16, 22c. World
Religions Picture Library/Alamy: 19t. Every attempt has been
made to clear copyright. Should there be any inadvertent omission
please apply to the publisher for rectification.

Franklin Watts is a division of Hachette Children's Books,
an Hachette UK company.
www.hachette.co.uk

# Contents

# A special birthday

## Christmas is a Christian festival.

Christians are people who follow a religion called Christianity. They live in countries all over the world and believe in one God.

Christians also believe that God sent Jesus Christ, His son, to the world to love and teach people and to save them from their sins. Christmas is the celebration of the birth of Jesus and is a happy time.

Children in Mexico celebrate Jesus's birthday with a special parade.

Christmas Day is celebrated once a year around the world. For many Christians it is celebrated on the 25th December, but some celebrate it on the 6th or 7th January.

Christians in Ethiopia celebrating Christmas with a procession on 7th January.

All over the world, families celebrate Christmas with a special meal.

Many people who are not Christian also celebrate Christmas. For everyone it is a time for families to come together. They share festive meals and give each other Christmas cards and gifts.

*At Christmas, we have a big family party at my nan's house, and I get to play with all my cousins.*
*Max, aged 10*

# The Christmas story

**At Christmas, Christians remember the story of Jesus's birth.**

The Christmas story tells how the Angel Gabriel appeared to Mary. The angel told her she was going to give birth to a baby boy, who would be the Son of God.

Mary was engaged to be married to Joseph. When she was about to have her baby, they had to travel to Bethlehem for a census.

> *" I did a drawing at school of the Angel Gabriel. "*
> *Nathan, aged 10*

▶ The Christmas story is shown in paintings, and in stained glass windows in churches. This window shows Mary and the baby Jesus.

When Mary and Joseph reached Bethlehem, they could not find anywhere to stay and had to shelter in a stable. Mary gave birth to Jesus in the stable and laid him in a manger.

An angel brought news of Jesus's birth to shepherds.

The Three Wise Men took the baby Jesus gifts of gold, frankincense and myrrh.

When Jesus was born, an angel appeared to shepherds in the fields near Bethlehem. The angel told them God's son had been born and the shepherds went to visit him.

Three Wise Men saw a new star in the sky, and followed it to find the baby Jesus, too.

# Advent

Advent is the time when Christians look forward to Jesus's birth.

It begins four Sundays before Christmas Day. Children can count down the days to Christmas with an Advent calendar.

An Advent calendar marking each day with a scene or symbol of Christmas.

Many Christians go to church during Advent, to sing carols and think about the Christmas story. Some carol services, called Christingles, are held by candlelight.

Children at a Christingle service. They hold an orange, which stands for the world, with a candle, which stands for the light Jesus brought into the world.

Nativity scenes are set up in churches, public places and homes to remind people of the Christmas story.

*"Mum lets me set up our Nativity scene every year. That's when I start to get excited because I know Christmas is coming."*
*Natalie, aged 9*

People send cards to each other during Advent to wish each other a happy Christmas.

**There are lots of different card designs to choose from.**

# Carols and plays

**The Christmas story is told in songs and plays.**

During Advent and Christmas, Christians sing carols and play music to celebrate Jesus's birth. Carol singers visit people at home, singing at the door and collecting money to give to poor and homeless people.

> **"** *I used to like singing carols around the crib when I was little.* **"**
> *Michelle, aged 9*

Children singing Christmas carols.

In schools in Britain and other countries, young children perform in Nativity plays, acting out the Christmas story. Their parents and friends come to watch them.

Children dressed as Mary, the Wise Men and the Angels for a school Nativity play.

In Mexico, children call at the houses of friends and neighbours to sing songs, and act out scenes from the Christmas story called posadas. The last house they visit takes them in, and after prayers they have a party.

A little girl carries a Nativity scene from house to house for the posadas in San Miguel, Mexico.

# Christmas decorations

Decorations make homes, streets, shops and churches look festive for Christmas.

People hang decorations and put up Christmas trees and fairy lights in homes, shops, schools and offices.

Candles and holly, ivy and mistletoe are traditional decorations in homes and churches.

Holly and ivy rings are hung from front doors to welcome friends at Christmas.

Baubles and other shiny decorations reflect the lights on Christmas trees.

Towns and cities have fairy lights and Christmas trees in their main streets and squares.

In many towns and cities, fairy or laser lights are hung over the main shopping streets.

A giant modern Christmas tree made from fairy lights.

*" My dad takes me to see the Christmas lights in town every year. They look really bright and cheerful. "*
Amy, aged 9

In southern India, Christian families light small oil lamps and put them on the flat roofs of their houses.

# Christmas Eve

**In some countries, the biggest celebrations take place on Christmas Eve.**

Christmas Eve is the night before Christmas. Many Christians go to church at midnight to celebrate the birth of Jesus.

At the midnight service many Christians welcome Christmas with a service called Mass or Holy Communion.

In Spain, people celebrate with street processions on Christmas Eve. They carry torches and play drums, tambourines and guitars.

A Christmas Eve procession carries a statue of Mary and Jesus through a village in southern Spain.

In European countries like Poland, Belgium and Sweden, families celebrate with a special meal on Christmas Eve.

In Poland, it is traditional to start eating when the first star appears in the sky.

In Poland, on Christmas Eve, families leave a place for the baby Jesus at the table.

# Going to church

**Many Christians go to church to celebrate Christmas.**

All around the world, churches are full on Christmas Day with people celebrating the birth of Jesus.

> **"** *We go to church on Christmas morning. My sister sings in the choir there.* **"**
>
> *Hannah, aged 9*

A village church in Fiji on Christmas Day.

A family service in the UK on Christmas Day.

Many churches hold family services on Christmas Day. Families listen to the Christmas story from the Bible and the priest or minister talks about the meaning of Christmas.

Children can join in singing carols around a crib. People say prayers to thank God for the birth of Jesus. They pray for peace on Earth, and for everyone who is poor, homeless or sick.

A priest leads a Christmas service in a church in Moscow, Russia.

# Christmas presents

**Christmas is a time for giving and receiving presents.**

The presents remind people of the gifts of gold, frankincense and myrrh that the Three Wise Men gave to Jesus. They also remind Christians that God gave the world the gift of His only son, Jesus.

Presents wrapped up to be opened on Christmas Day.

There are different traditions on who brings children their Christmas presents. In many countries, it may be Father Christmas, who is also called Santa Claus or Saint Nicholas, who brings the presents.

Santa Claus visiting children on a beach in Australia.

20

In Germany, it may be the baby Jesus who brings presents, in Spain, the Wise Men, and in Italy, an old woman called La Befana.

This is a model of La Befana. Italian tradition says she brings gifts on the eve of 6th January.

Presents may be left in Christmas stockings, shoes or boots by a fireplace. Sometimes, they are put under the Christmas tree.

Christmas stockings filled with presents ready for opening.

**❝** *On Christmas morning I always find a sock at the bottom of my bed filled with satsumas, nuts, and very small presents. I get bigger presents later in the day.* **❞**
*Callum, aged 9*

# Festive food

## Christmas is a time for feasting with family and friends.

At midday or in the evening, many families sit down for a big Christmas meal together. In the Czech Republic, even pets and farm animals share the Christmas food.

Australian families eat their Christmas dinner in the sun, as Christmas falls in their summer.

In Britain, the Christmas meal is often roast turkey or goose, with roast potatoes and vegetables. In Portugal, they eat salted dried codfish and potatoes, and in Nova Scotia, people eat lobster for Christmas dinner.

Lobster is a favourite Christmas dish in Nova Scotia, Canada.

People eat special sweet dishes, too.

In Britain, there is often a Christmas pudding. Many countries also have a cake and mince pies made with dried fruits.

**" Mum makes a Christmas cake a few weeks before Christmas. She says it tastes better that way. "**

Tanya, aged 10

In Italy they eat a special cake called panettone.

In Germany they eat stollen, a cake filled with dried fruit and marzipan.

23

# Family time

**For many people, Christmas is a family time.**

People travel home to spend Christmas with their family. Trains, planes and roads get busy in the days before Christmas.

Three generations of a family gather together to open their Christmas presents around the tree.

Families find many different ways to have fun at Christmas. Many families play games together at home.

*" We always have crackers at Christmas. You pull them and they make a loud bang. You find a hat to wear and a small toy or game inside. "*

Lauren, aged 9

In the USA, families go to watch special Christmas parades.

A Christmas parade in Virginia, USA.

At Christmas in Finland, people like to remember their loved ones who have died. They take candles to put on their family graves.

Candles brighten up graves in Finland at Christmas.

# The message of Christmas

**Christmas is a time for giving and caring. It is also a time for praying for peace on Earth.**

At Christmas, Christians remember that Jesus taught them to love and care for each other, and to help those who are in need.

On Christmas Day, many people give their time to help others, by taking food or gifts to people who are old, sick or poor.

A boy takes a Christmas gift to an elderly neighbour.

These children are receiving toys collected for poor families by the police service.

Children help serve Christmas meals to homeless people at a soup kitchen.

At shelters and church halls, people cook and serve Christmas meals for the poor and homeless.

Around the world, Christians pray for an end to war and for forgiveness and peace in all countries. This was the message that the angels sang to the shepherds at Jesus's birth.

*66 At the club I go to after church on Sundays, we wrapped up boxes of food to take to old people who live nearby. 99*

*Daniel, aged 10*

# Glossary

**Advent** the four weeks before Christmas.

**Bethlehem** the town, south of Jerusalem in Israel, where Jesus was born.

**Bible** the holy book of Christianity.

**Carol** a song sung at Christmas to celebrate the birth of Jesus.

**Census** a count of people. In Roman times, people and their property were counted for taxation.

**Christingle** a candle held in an orange, which is decorated with a red ribbon and other fruit or nuts.

**Communion** when Christians eat blessed bread and wine. They do this in memory of Jesus and of all that he did for them. Many Christians believe Jesus is present after the bread and wine are blessed. The service in which communion takes place is called by a number of names, such as the Mass, Holy Communion, the Last Supper and the Eucharist.

**Crib** a baby's bed, with high sides.

**Frankincense** a perfume that comes from trees.

**Manger** a long box that holds hay for feeding animals.

**Myrrh** a perfume that comes from trees.

**Nativity play** a play that tells the story of Jesus's birth.

**Nativity scene** a model of the scene in the stable when Jesus was born.

**Sins** bad or wrong actions, thoughts or behaviour.

# Christianity

Christianity is one of the world's main religions. There are over one billion Christians around the world. Christians believe in one God, who made everything in the universe.

## Jesus Christ

Christians follow the teachings of Jesus Christ, who lived about 2,000 years ago. They believe that Jesus is the Son of God and He was sent to save people from sin and death. Jesus taught people to love and praise God as their Father, and to love and care for others. Jesus was crucified (killed on a wooden cross). Christians believe He came back to life on the third day after His death and that everyone who believes in Him will live again after they die.

## Christian lives

Christians are christened or baptised to show that they believe in Jesus. They follow the teachings of the holy Bible, and praise God with hymns, readings and prayers.

## Branches

Christians belong to different branches. These include the Roman Catholic, Orthodox, Anglican, Pentecostal, Methodist, Baptist branches and many others.

## Festivals

Christmas is an important festival for most Christians, but there are many other important Christian festivals in the year, for example Easter.

# Index